Light Still, Light Turning

Yvonne Baker

Published by Cinnamon Press
www.cinnamonpress.com

ISBN 978-1-78864-172-2

British Library Cataloguing in Publication Data. A CIP record for this book can be obtained from the British Library.

Designed and typeset in Bodini by Cinnamon Press. Cover design by Adam Craig © Adam Craig.

Cinnamon Press is represented by Inpress.

Acknowledgements

Thank you to the hard working editors who accepted these poems over the years, sometimes in earlier versions and with a different title. *Orbis*: 'Reflection'; *Coffee House Poetry*, Cinnamon Press: 'Walking Boots', 'This isn't me', 'Tourist'; *Poetry & All THAT Jazz*: 'Unearthed'; *Artemis POETRY*: 'The face of my mother', 'Camera', 'Anatomy lesson'; *Equinox*: 'Closing in'; *Quattrocento*: 'Floating'; Frogmore Press: 'Dear Vincent'; *Green Fuses*, published by Dempsey and Dwindle: 'Beginnings'; *Washed with Noon*, published by Dempsey and Dwindle: 'Dark sky', 'Double Exposure'; *Liminal*, A collection of poetry, by Chichester Stanza: 'Waiting for morning', 'This winter rain is how it is', 'Nightfall', 'Flying above the clouds'.

Grateful thanks are due to Mimi Khalvati for her wisdom and advice on writing poetry, and I am particularly indebted to Myra Schneider for her encouragement, close reading and guidance over many years. Warmest thanks to Jan Fortune for her encouragement, mentoring, and careful editing. My appreciation also to all at Cinnamon Press for the beautifully printed books and for accepting my work.

Yvonne Baker is married with three sons and five grandchildren. She worked for many years as a teacher in primary education, and later as a headteacher and religious education adviser. She has been published in print and on-line magazines and placed in competitions. Her poems have been included in Second Light, Paper Swans, Emma Press and Poetry Space anthologies. She belongs to several poetry groups: Chichester Stanza, Taking Your Work Further, Kith Poets and Second Light Network, all of which offer support and friendship.Her poetry explores the relationship between the outer and inner experience and how this can reveal hidden emotions and feelings. Her debut poetry pamphlet, *Tree Light*, was a winner in the Cinnamon Pamphlet Prize 2022 and her debut collection, *Love Haunts in Shades of Blue*, won the Cinnamon Literature Prize. Her most recent collection with Cinnamon Press was *Backwards, forwards across the sea.*

Contents

For Mo

with love and thanks for all the years of friendship

Light Still, Light Turning

Double exposure

The house, perches on the corner,
its paint blistering, grass-seed whirling.

You pass in the car, watch a neglected memory
disintegrate without sentiment.

But the past leaves a shadow on the lens.

Superimposed on the image of
the low-rise flats now squatting in its place

are snaps that show your mother squinting in the sun,
father kneeling on the grass beside you,

baby brother laughing with the woman downstairs—
ghosts who won't be distanced.

They smile confidently in the front garden
that slopes towards the dark privet, the busy road,

as though the year's wheel has stopped.

Unfolding

i)

behind the glass of the photo
time is still

the sea's movement a ploughed field

ii)

light breathes into the room
touches bowls and jugs
with history unrelated to you

what you can see outside the window
happened eight minutes ago—

measure of the sun's
reach to Earth

iii)

darkness under soil and rock
holds millennia in its depths

time journeys over
gravity's hills and valleys

iv)

in the photo all time is hidden—

the ancient village emerging
from a reservoir after drought

bell tower and bridge
glinting in the sun

will be eventually
submerged under water and night

v)

looking at the photo
of the first house you lived in

the small child that was you
exploring forgotten places

illusive as shadows of lost light

The face of my mother

The young girl, straight hair pinned back with a slide,
hand-me-down dress, has gone. Now your hair is permed

under a hat curved like a rainbow. Your coat has a fur collar.
Perhaps this is an attempt to imagine yourself as one

of the women who flicker across a world of silver light,
while you sit in the darkness watching their story.

A studio study, you are posed in front of a blank screen.
The light is subtle, glides over your half-parted lips.

Your eyes retreat to your inner world. A chrysalis moment,
you are becoming—not yet

married with children, not yet touched by the sadness
that comes from being alive. A moment waiting

to emerge, flutter on, to the time when you are the mother
who cleans houses to provide for your children

and offers me your chocolates when, at sixteen,
I sit on your bed, my mascara tears catching the light.

Camera

Maybe she's just startled by the blink of the shutter
as she grasps the ears of a stone rabbit,

nearly as large as herself.
Standing in a well-tended garden,

in one of the houses her mother cleans,
she stares back solemnly in her stripy dress.

You'd like to think that she is looking
with curiosity at the world.

It's the lens that drafts her forgotten self in light,
she doesn't remember the day.

The future behind trees

i)

On an afternoon in a century out of focus,

small girls in smocks
explore a garden outside a school-house.

Behind the trees, sky—a muslin curtain pulled tight—
conceals an autumn morning yet to dawn.

ii)

Along a faint horizon girls—not yet thought of—
amble towards a building with gleaming glass.

You can't see yourself among them.

So much still needs to happen—
wars, births—before that image is developed.

iii)

Today stretches impossibly far from
the scene with glinting windows

and you are at the vanishing point for those girls in the garden.
They have faded into fragile light.

You gaze at a cloud-bank, think about distance.

First selfie

You snap the wind-torn self,
face-naked, nose reddened by cold,
trying to empty your face.

You think about what this hides,
what it reveals, the same way
you wonder at the arranged features

caught each morning under the ice-glaze
of glass and light, the self who
witnesses it, the self that you can no more

see than you can see your eyes.

Reflection

Your fingers trace the neckline.
Slipping the hanger off the rail, the tag
brushes your wrist.

You stand before the mirror,
pressing the dress against you,
its shoulders against yours—just to see.

Head slightly angled, you wear
your mirror face so no one
can guess what you're thinking—

soft Peruvian cotton, tiny buttons,
the colour that lights up your skin.
There would be no harm.

Cubicle door clicks shut.
The dress clings like perfume,
possibilities tissue thin.

And there you are, the two of you
undecided who you are, sliding
into grey streets edgy with rain.

Your reflection, not knowing
limitations of glass, avoids you.
You pull your coat closer.

This isn't me

Marilyn, Andy Warhol

kitsch yellow hair
rictus slash—chilli-red—
a stare
grainy as newsprint
repeating
        repeating

        who is it
transfixed
shadow-smudged
in this eerie vacuum?

day flickers
against night
        rows
        columns
columns and rows
still frames
        over and over

am I here? still?

The Sale of the Shadow

After Kirchner

In the New Year, your shadow
began to irritate. Midsummer,
as light deepened, it was unbearable.
Flat days, or when rain
washed away the light,
it might disappear but never for long.

Once when you took it to the cinema
it skulked by the smiling usherette, dissolved
in the feathery blackness
that brushed your skin,
then, as you passed the popcorn kiosk,
it rejoined you.

Finally, slipping the shadow
from your shoulders, you draped
its chamois darkness on a hanger,
took it to a car boot sale,
sold it to a man, with a splintered smile,
It flapped piteously.

Sometimes, at twilight,
you sense from the corner of your eye,
a wisp, something huddled.
So you pick up the darkness
from the corner,
            wrap it around you.

Unnoticed

Under your misremembered memories,
there's a stillness.

You rarely listen to it.

Elusive, in the cells of your body,
perfectly camouflaged—

a motionless woodcock
hiding from daylight,

its dry-leafed plumage overlooked
on the forest floor

in the silence
of the yellow-grey light of rain.

Anatomy lesson

After Rembrandt

How confident you look Doctor Tulp
with the light of attention on you
as you explain the secrets of the body.

One hand lifts a crimson tendon
while the other gestures to explain
the bend and stretch of fingers.

The dead man is mapped out before us
but our eyes are drawn towards you
the renowned explorer; probing

pathways of veins, you return
from the body's subterranean lands
with insight of its dark caverns

and the canals that carry life
but perhaps less clear
about what it means.

You believe the soul is buried
in the pineal gland and has left—
a change in body weight told you that.

Yet despite your years of truth-seeking
your only certainty is that life has gone.
Its why and where require a different path

and your scalpel is no help.
You must enter that silent cave
where there are no obvious answers

just small steps on a pilgrimage
through darkness, searching
in a country you have always known.

Time gallery

As you gaze at a painting,
days, years, millennia, slip into
a sink hole of a deeper time.

The gleam on a silver jug,
the pale dress of Whistler's lady,
are weighty with lead, carry
a burden of theft from the land.

Vermeer's white-walled room,
glowing with inner light, is
gleaned from alabaster, quartz,
gouged from darkness.

The ochre sleeves of a milkmaid
are fashioned from yellow clay,
while cinnabar yields vermillion
for a courtier's skirt—

minerals, all formed
when Earth was still young,
pounded to dust, as the sea
grinds stones to sand.

Iron pyrite, once suspended in
lapis lazuli, is discarded, so stars
no longer shine in a blue veil.

Between times

The Mistress and the Maid, Vermeer

The woman about to take
a letter from the maid,
is caught between now
and what might be.

While in my room,
the flowers I bought
are withering with
the quietness of dust.

Soon, she will
shift her pose, the artist
put down his brush,
but, for now, the woman,
her finger on her chin,
stays poised in stillness.

On my window, rain skims
like the weave of slub silk.
I imagine space-time as
a bolt of cloth, my life
woven with the woman's.

She waits in a moment,
neither day or night—
her dress, bright against
the darkness, in her hair
pearls of light.

Closing in

The room is familiar—

a coffee stain on the couch,
a reflection curved
on the vase holding
crimson tulips

In the mirror,
submerged in
tarnished sunlight,
a woman
swaddled
in a dressing gown,
bends over
a book.

The air, stale with her story,
spools towards
the wrong side
of the room
through
the open window
to an emulsioned

sky, arched high, tight
against the rain.

Tourist

i) Ernest Hemingway's House, Havana

Buffalo heads, glassy-eyed, stare
as though startled to find themselves
hanging here. Across the room
a typewriter that seems small
for so many words, and a narrow bed,
counterpane smoothed.
For a moment it almost seems real.

But on the desk, memories
are pressed under glass
and the library book, unreturned
since 1929, is only an artefact.
The only signs of life are birds,
tail feathers fanned, hopping
in the dense heat of the garden,
the jostle of carob and palms.

In bright air, an empty pool,
sky-coloured, gapes.

ii) As you peer in at your window

dusk slowly begins to gather,
erases the garden.

Your reflection disappears
from the glass.

This is how easily you can vanish
from your life.

Without you the room resembles
a gallery closed for the afternoon—

a cobalt vase, grey-stone elephant,
four generations of Matryoshka dolls,

exhibited on the shelves.
One day, when the room is dismantled,

they will continue their separate ways.

Floating

After Bonnard

I will give you a room of Naples yellow, he said,
decorate the bathroom with tiles of grey blue,
the dining room with Japanese woodcuts,
paint the cupboard red.
You can have solitude while I have light.

Of course, I am never alone.
Pierre is forever observing—
bowls of fruit, flowers, the fireplace gold
in the afternoon sun—
capturing the light.

Then he starts on me. I can't sit
at the table, have a bath;
he waits for me at every turn.
While he sketches, I lie here—
a water lily floating in cooling dreams.

My hair greys, mouth sours. But
under Pierre's gaze, my skin still has
the bloom he first saw. My little dog sleeps
on a sparkling mosaic floor.
The walls glow in our closed world.

Holding on

The studio is also part of my painting, Piet Mondrian
Mondrian and his Studios, Tate Liverpool, 2004

Look at Pieter standing there
an almost perfect vertical,
with our parents, the boys and I,
fixed in sepia, inseparable.

But Piet squeezed
my hand, whispered he would escape,
one day become a painter.

Mother always in bed, Father at church,
we children crouched around
the choking stove. Piet sat apart,
pencils in rows on the scrubbed table.

His hand slipped mine when he left
for the Academy. Now he's in Paris,
in a studio near the station.

He writes he can see the tracks,
criss-crossed outside his window.
His world pared to pure colours, and white,
cut with black, he is happy in his painting.

But I remember
a small boy, with a shy smile,
the way he grasped my hand so tightly.

Fountain House

Anna Akhmatova's home in St Petersburg during World War II and Stalin's terror years

i)
The rooms are artfully arranged

the samovar on the shelf,
the photographs, the shawl
displayed across a chair,

the bed Lev built for himself
squeezed into the corridor,

the inkstand that you used
writing all those letters
for Lev's release,

the ashtray where you burnt
your poems before
they could be discovered.

The poems still flicker in the flames.

ii)
Before coming here we queued
at the visa office to deliver

our application forms with the details
of our place of birth and work, parents,

places visited. all dated, ordered, stamped.
I wondered how a country, so in love

with poetry, could be so bureaucratic.
I thought of you, the endless letters

begging Stalin to release your son.
Sadness, you said, is a prison

and you refused to be interned,
You queued for fifteen years.

Dear Vincent

Irises, Vincent van Gogh

Theo van Gogh wrote constantly to Vincent during the painter's lifetime.

Sometimes as I begin to write to you
I almost stop, knowing it's too late,
then carry on—unsure what else to do
and habit has its own momentum.
Those irises so full of life and air
still haunt the corners of my dreams.
Painting, you said, would keep you sane
but (this thought still wakes me in the night)
despite your hopefulness I should have seen
how one white iris veers towards the edge
and stands alone amongst a crowd of blue.
I couldn't protect you. I think I always knew
words were futile, wouldn't take away your pain
but, even as I hesitate, I start to write again.

Distracted

Ophelia, John Everett Millais

by the clarity of each willow leaf, each
blade of grass, it would be easy
to forget the girl is drowning—

not to notice the small fish
slipping from under the mat of weed
in the darkened water

or not to discern that it is yourself
who is sinking below crow flowers
and poppies, unaware

of what has disappeared
                in a flick of silver.

Pausing

A Courtyard in Delft, Pieter de Hooch

Your stillness might mean you're content
to look out from the narrow hallway
that shelters your gaze.

Or maybe your thoughts are elsewhere,
your maid and child bystanders,
their chatter fading as quietness pools,
while you catch the sun on your apron.

Perhaps you consider your future is enclosed
in the well-swept courtyard behind you.
To want more than this might mean
to lose all you hold dear.

Or are you thinking about the blue arc
of the sky with its endless possibilities?
If only you would step forward.

it's always now

i)

you dream of a house
that once was now

you're constructing a corridor
in the narrow hallway

there is only grey light inside

you wonder if you have built a space
between moments

ii)

when you watch
light turning
you think you see time

iii)

you think you can
circumvent time's drift

only to find
the photo faded in the sun
poem forgotten

iv)

unnoticed
time holds past and future
in each moment

as you step into
        the empty page
                you carry your life

v)

as a hundred million neutrinos
pass seamlessly in each instant
through your body

so time flows through everything

vi*)*

light dazzles with brilliance

it turns the year's wheel until
fixed in pixel or on paper

vii)

the crystal heart
your mother gave you
grows heavy in your hand
her name and yours
etched in light

viii)

you could fold this poem
smaller and smaller
only to find its creases
still disturb your dreams
sharply

Beginnings

i)

Through grass, crisp with frost,
the walk to the shed is cold.
The door opens to the warm smell
of varnished wood, the quietness
of neglected brushes and paints.

I dip brush into water, pigment.
Colours weep into the paper,
something unlooked for emerges.

ii)

On the cusp of a new year,
my thoughts, overwintering
between anxiety and hope,
begin to push into grey air.

When all is silent, safe from
frayed plans, future uncertainty,
a green shoot, opens—
maybe on a morning bright
with unseasonable warmth,
or on one cold enough for snow.

This winter rain is how it is

The place where children scraped their knees is no longer here.
It has been changed by time and the children grown:

In the continuous rain the garden is a landscape of mud,
where footprints are washed away, birds no longer sing,

and the squirrel, grown fat with nuts put out for the blue tits,
has disappeared. There's a hesitation in the way things are.

You tell yourself that there's always a shift, that goldfinch
and wood-mouse will be here for your great grandchildren.

In this time of turmoil, you hope the wheel will turn.
It's what always happened. You listen for the wren's shrill call.

rejoice in the broken

for the coffee cup that slipped
from your hand and smashed
for the friend whose gift it was
now no longer close
          for the turquoise bowl
its glaze inexplicably chipped
the rug with weave grown thin
          and the washing machine
chugging its last breath as the clock
that was a present from the dead
stopped with its hands in prayer

you'd like to be grateful
for seismic shifts that pushed
the plates of your old world
into a life you didn't ask for
          those plans torn on the journey
when the road was too narrow
and double parked
          the way threads of hope
cut your heart as you hung on
brittle nails threatening to break
          bruise-coloured nights
you almost drown in sadness
because you never learned to swim

rejoice instead that you are trying
to learn to forgive yourself
for wasting the gift of days
          for the time you failed
to notice the bird dying at your feet
because you were staring at clouds
the way you felt useless
when anxiety encircled the hours

          and your frozen watchfulness
at the hollow of dust
standing in place of a forest

you think about how
everything is gathered up to be
mended or remade
and there are days
when you can see the fault lines
gleaming with lacquer and gold
see how sharing the world's sorrow
is precious in understanding life

other times fog
muffles the light and you walk
through deadening silence
feeling nothing

you need to forgive that too

variations in the fall of light

the evening warm light long
you bookmark the moment
anticipate the next chapter

          it's dark outside the door
          the cold air brittle as glass
          the wind stutters in the leaves

between pages a moth's wings
are embedded in the print

          rusty hinges squeak a warning
          you may lose your self
          in the unknown

feelings pass in a flick of paper
this is not a stone book

          some pages are only bearable
          when they are closed

you are writer and reader
free to change punctuation
interpret the text

          the pages of the years
          flap in a wind grey with rain

the spine is strong even
although it's creased with wear

          the text is growing faint
          soon it'll be washed blank
          by the downpour

another night evaporates
in the light of day

          peony petals bleed their redness
          grow thin as they alter from
          deep pink to apricot to pale lemon

marbled end pages
translucent and fragile
describe a different beauty

The problem with light

She was sixteen, he seventeen, a party of sorts—
almost midsummer, the sun invasive.

Someone tried to block the brightness, but light
blew between the thin curtains.

She remembered him framed in the doorway,
thought him quite good looking.

He only had eyes for his girlfriend.
She said it was indifference at first sight.

Years later, at a time when days were shorter,
light softer, they met at another party.

He said he'd wanted to ask her out for some time.
She said she hadn't noticed.

Seasons circled—they decided to marry in winter.

Waiting for morning

The room's sloped ceiling
holds night in the crease
by the window.

Darkness freezes time.

You don't want to return
to that dream—
the one of travelling on a train,

missing your station, unsure
where you are heading,
where you came from.

Neither do you want to lie awake.

On a slipstream of thought
you arrive in a garden overcome
by the weight of the sun,

where you search for shade.
A night-heron perches on a rock
in the creek, watching the ripple

of water for the possibility of fish.
Each of you aware only
of this particular time and place—

the moment deepening like sleep.

Night fall

On the small island,
somewhere west
of your memories, with
its day that never finishes,
stars are faint in the almost night.

There is a brightness
over the fish farm in the bay.
Salmon, unable to sleep,
churn the water round
and round.

You have forgotten
how, in winter, you long
for the lengthening of days,
Now you crave for darkness
to frost your eyes with sleep.

The tantalising line
of light around the horizon,
intrusive as a streetlamp,
illuminates the bed. Salmon
continue to swim.

Breaking free

Mu
Xim
under
house arrest
used strips of paper
provided for his confession
to paint ink-landscapes of sullen mountains, waterfalls.
And so, for a while, escaped the Cultural Revolution, constraints of time and space.

Dancing

Lately I've been thinking about how atoms,
over time, reject order to dance in a space,
speeding up as moments tick by—
the way a thought might begin in
pinprick-stillness, spill out to change a life.

Even the universe is in flux
as it spreads, chills, heads towards death.
And I think of Schrödinger, who
occasionally thought about these things.

I imagine him towards the end of his life,
perhaps with his cat asleep on his lap,
while he muses on how, as we age,
disorder ensues in our cells, until death
moves in, our atoms joining that tarantella.

Cantrip

In the snapshot of the night—
ghosts of galaxies flicker
a valediction, while black holes
singing in B flat, open
into another time and space.

In my eye is another time
and place. Behind its black
centre—memories, dreams,
conjure songs of other worlds,
in the snapshot of the night.

Flying over Google Earth

You skim above your childhood,
loss and longing hold your hands,
as you visit the landscape of early life,
the house you've never missed.

It's no longer there.

Memory-borne, you search for
a glimpse of your father hurrying
home, a small girl in a pink-rose dress,
riding her birthday tricycle.

You're learning to walk across
indentations you once made in time.
Today the space overflows
with other lives, untouched by yours.

All that remains is a trace of how you once felt.

Soaring to the place that was always home,
you touch down on grass, try to catch
sight of a girl staring at the stars,
her life stretched out. But she's gone.

An ache grips you.
You long to see a face in a window,
someone who might smile
in recognition. Perhaps wave.

You have learned how each
new day peels something else away—
lost keys, a treasured vase, your hearing,
people who were always there.

There's no going back—

only a journey to faraway depths and edges.
Earth orbits the sun, leaves behind
those dark-reflecting windows,
where all you can see is your face.

Behind windows

Evenings would often find him
in the car. Just sitting.

In winter darkness was his protection.
Summer, cooking smells drifted

through windows, Perry Como softly
crooned *Magic Moments*.

Boys would tap on the driver's window,
circle the car, shake it from side-to side.

His thin face creased under a check cap,
he stared at the windscreen

long after the street lights came on.
I don't remember his name.

Once, his wife screeched from the shadows
to *stop this nonsense* and *come inside*.

Although the evening was warm,
there was a volley of slamming windows.

Remembering a future that didn't happen

My father sits on the couch that has become tired with time. He is leaning forward, as if with the particular anxiety that stems from imagination, his veined hand with its missing finger tense. Through a gap in the cotton curtains, constellations faintly shine.

My mother and brother are absent, already part of a larger sky. I tell him this is the wrong order that he will leave before all of us. We wait together in borrowed light that washes over walls.

flying above the clouds

the white landscape stretches
to the edge of blue

its uneven surface somewhere
you might drag a sleigh

an opening reveals
a lake of sky

distance
makes desolation attractive

immersed in cloud
perspective changes

you no longer know
where you are going

where you are
whiteness veils your view of the world

even the window can't
soften its effects

emerging
the constant sky is clear

Slievenamon

County Tipperary

to a child it seemed an enchanted country

shaped by mist

a sky-coloured

place of longing

years later

climbing

its road

the streams and sandstone were beautiful

views

breath-taking
breath-
giving

I longed for Slievenamon

its silent clouds
drifting

blue-shadowed

by distance

Walking boots

For Mike

in a petrified moment
you are

balancing across a chasm

suspended

by slats and frayed ropes

on your back a heavy rucksack
your bead bent
in concentration
is touched by light

and you
who do not believe in any god

put one worn boot
in front of the other—

an act of faith

these boots will take you
to other places

grip rainy mountain sides
sound their mantra on solitary roads

at times you'll wonder where
you're heading
but
in this moment

you step with certainty

out

onto a causeway of peeled air

Chichester Canal

We walk along the waterway,
where willow-herb and red-mace grow—

the clouds unmoving.

Moorhens skim the bright green weed.
Across black water a coot is calling—

a cracked electric bell.

Surfers

St Ouwen's Baye, Jersey

From behind the windscreen, you watch the figures
run across the pale beach towards the sea.

Reflections quivering in pools of sky,
they pass through cobalt shallows to deeper blue.

Watch how they lay boards on white turmoil that rears
and bucks, trusting the wave will support them

that their balance won't fail. You think about
being immersed in distant grey-green depths

without a board, which requires a different courage.
Dozing in the sun, you haven't even left the car.

Waves

are not water
but the energy of the wind
that disturbs the air
                curling
        dipping
pushing the ruffled skin of the sea
so that
it reflects waves of light
        sparkles

and trillions of bubbles
                vibrate
their song
        in fingers
of air and water
        pulled
                down
        by waves
of gravity

while hidden currents
beneath
        move along
a different path
        at their own speed

everything is in flux
held in a pattern of change
        you sometimes
think of as time

in this quiet harbour
the waves   energy spent
lap the the stone walls
of the quay

you watch their almost stillness
among a lamentation of swans

Unearthed

Oseberg ship, Viking Museum, Bygdøy, Oslo.

In its belly open to the sky,
the remains of two women
are swaddled in soil.

All that is left are their delicate bones,
teeth furrowed by wear.

Their grave goods are stolen,
identities windblown across
the past's great ocean.

Existence doesn't ask for names.
The women continue their last voyage.

Broighter boat

The National Museum of Ireland

A shell of gold
its oars—wire-thin—
dip and lift as it skims
land and water.
A votive offering
carried to a sea-deity
over waves of lost light,
the myth of appeasing
an angry universe clinging
in its wake,
            until moored
in this glass harbour.

Undertide

i)

afloat and lost in life's particulars
you are unable to touch the seabed—

the list-of-things-to-do
the watery spring that dissolves

your resolution of a daily walk—
life's shape makes you feel uneasy

ii)

a glass of water shot through with light
reflects details of the room

the pattern of the coaster
on the planes of the tumbler is jumbled

with pale walls—
their strangeness part of home

you drink the water savouring
its metallic taste its silken texture

feel the coldness that lingers
in your throat

while the glass grows warm
in your hand

iii)

this place and time are your ocean floor

the familiarity of its sift of sands
salt taste of its currents

tidal moods
are part of the gift of belonging

its surface tension bears a sheen of light

Summer Isle

i)

I arrive in a tiny boat, with food for a week.
Julia, wife of Tiberius, banished to Pandataria

for five years, was forbidden wine and company.
Tanera Mor, has no access to television or the internet.

A small island can soon seem claustrophobic,
the water enclose as surely as walls, so I centre

on the rubrics of coffee making, the ritual walk,
rather than follow the narrow road into my thoughts.

ii)

Habits are comforting. On the second day I settle
in the same chair as yesterday, think about how daily tasks

mask the risks of tomorrow, how fragile this notion is.
The clatter of bucket, the peat-brown water fetched to clean,

are not a safeguard against a sudden squall that transforms
the mood of the sea and, in a breath, changes everything.

By the old herring station, is a garden turned
wild, a shell of a house. Women once gossiped here,

unaware that their men would not return.
Only the chimney stands, like routine, it's last to weaken.

iii)

Sitting on the shore, my mind takes a different path.
I think about how air and spirit have the same root,

how breath is the first and the final sound in life.
I begin to picture a hermit, in his bee-hive cell,

inhaling atoms present at the beginning of time.
Of course, my fictional monk wouldn't think of this.

Instead, he might lose himself in wonder at the breathless
fall of blue from sky to sea, how day stretches here.

Or sit in a night of luminous darkness, with hunger
past understanding, for which he has risked everything.

as above so below

sky above air

sea below water

existing in parallel
segued in clouds

a small ritual

scooping
the loam-brown particles
you savour the sharp sweetness
of their smell

listen to the water
bubbling as it warms then
                                        dripping
into the grey morning
reflected in the glass jug

your mug
cobalt like a late spring sky
round with promise
fits your cupped hand

the gleam of sun on its glaze
highlights the circle-pattern
of the potter's wheel

embodies its maker's touch
the way a line of poetry
holds a writer's breath

add milk to your drink until
it's the colour of river silt
leaving a residue
in mouth and throat as you
swallow the bitter darkness

allow the remaining dregs
to disappear into the sink
return to river and sea

rinsed of its scent and taste
the mug
open to the rest of the day
fills with sky that's beginning
to lighten the room.

Communion

In the breath of winter
as it enters a wall,

or the salt kiss
between sea and marsh,

the world is in love with itself.

Intimacy makes the ordinary sacred
a cloth, a book, a cup, bread.

In praise of a solar eclipse

Nebraska, August 2017

For the sun, whose radiance
stretches over the vastness of the plains.
        For the passion of its heat.
        For the shadow-bite of the moon
that traces a path across the amber fire,
shields the Earth—
as when God turned his back
to protect Moses
from a love he didn't understand.
        For the cold shudder of the day,
the colour of sleep that silvers
the sky, the faded birdsong
circling the horizon.
        For the the moment
when the cleaving of night from day
becomes meaningless.
        For the solitude of loss
in the deathlike darkness, deep
as the Great Silence
of the flatlands between Compline
and Lauds.
        For the diamond halo of the moon,
a glimpse in the Stygian day
of the sun's glory.
        For the illusion of seeing the sun face to face.

www.ingramcontent.com/pod-product-compliance
Lightning Source LLC
LaVergne TN
LVHW090134160826
845673LV00017B/2471

* 9 7 8 1 7 8 8 6 4 1 7 2 2 *